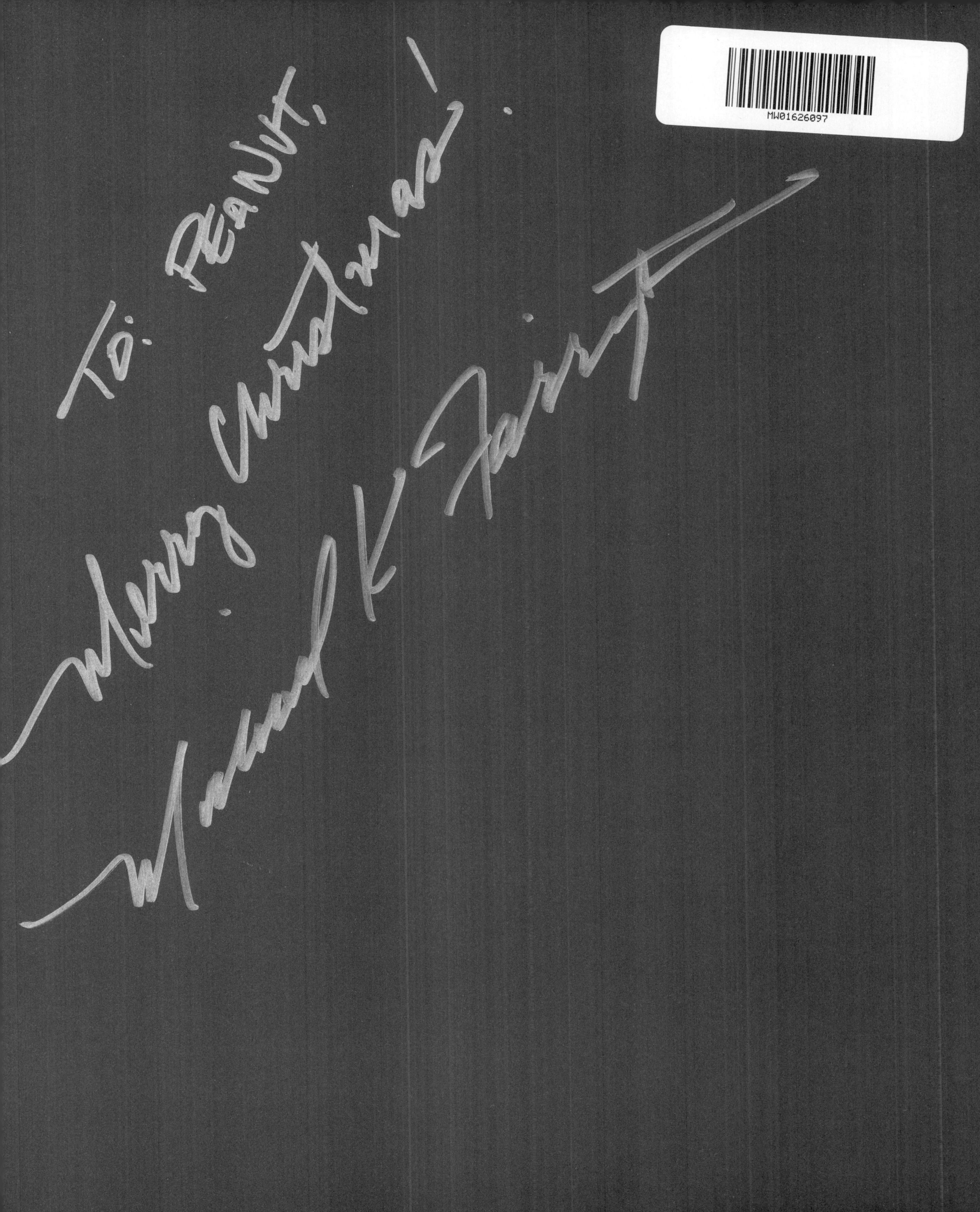
MW01626097
To: PEANUT,
Merry Christmas!

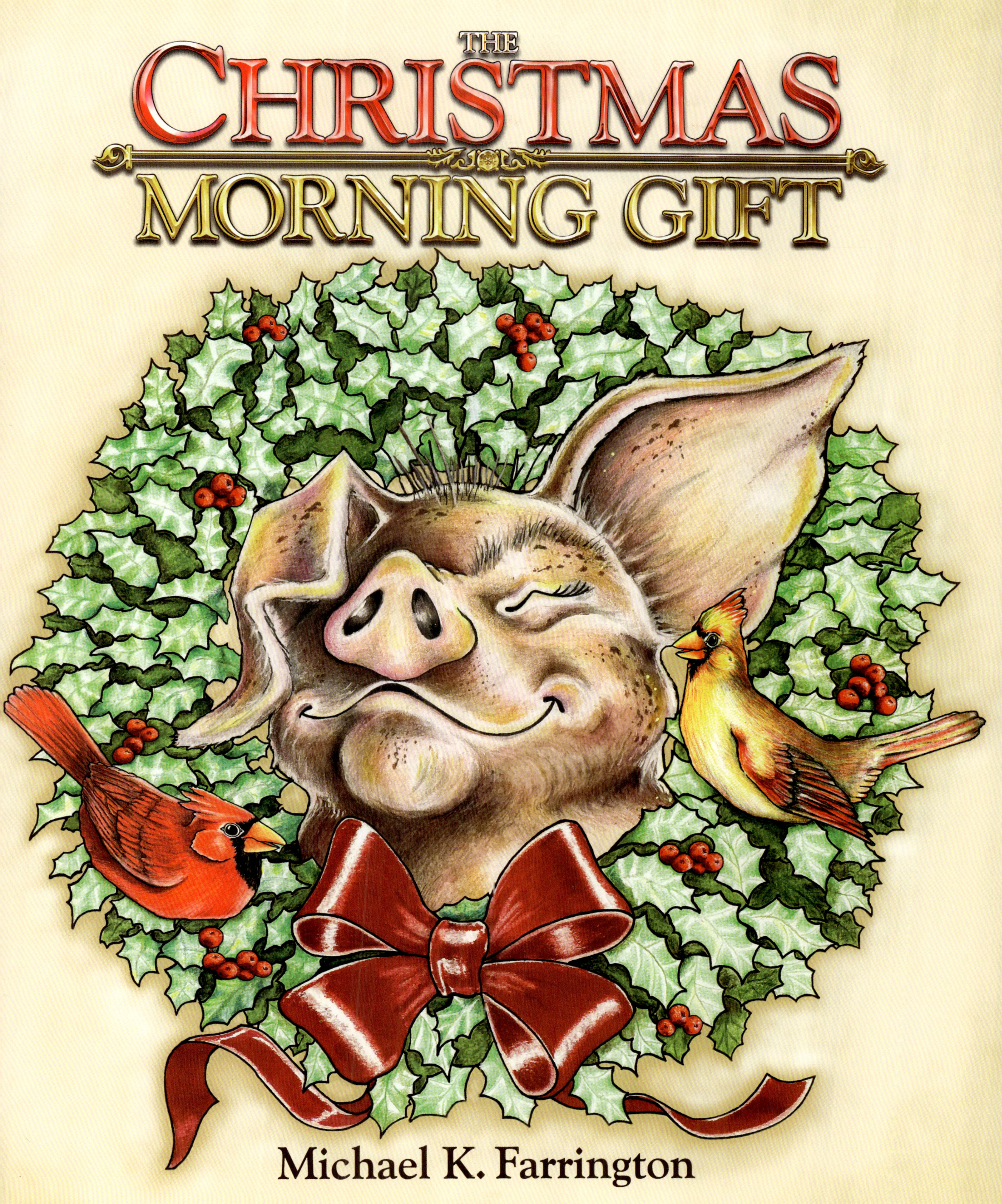
THE
CHRISTMAS
MORNING GIFT
Michael K. Farrington

The Christmas Morning Gift
Michael K. Farrington

www.TheChristmasMorningGift.com
www.michaelkfarrington.com

Illustrations: Michael K. Farrington
Editor: Nancy C. Allen
Text Layout: Karen K. Christoffersen
Title Design: Anthony Molina

Library of Congress Cataloging-in-Publication Data: Pending
Library of Congress Control Number 2011918566

ISBN 978-1-60645-084-0
10 9 8 7 6 5 4 3 2 1

PRINTED IN CHINA

Michael K. Farrington

It was Christmas morning and the brisk, now distant, night air had given way to the life-giving warmth of the sun. The shimmering glow of light was soft and pure as it trickled down through a small crack at the top of the barn door. It added an angelic charm reminiscent of the very first Christmas Day in another stable, so far away.

All night the animals had slumbered until one fleeting sunbeam reached the very tip of the rosy-speckled pig's snout, and he twitched and stirred in the warmth, feeling refreshed and renewed.

Today is going to be a grand Christmas Day, he thought.

By nature he was shy and unassuming, and the uniqueness of his rosy-speckled appearance brought him constant, unwanted attention. Nonetheless, the other animals were drawn to him because of his kind, unpretentious nature.

Shouts of joy and laughter rang out from the horse-drawn sleigh as the farmer and his wife enjoyed the solitary splendor of the freshly fallen snow. It had been a year of hope and cheer, and their thoughts focused on the blessings of the season. They could almost hear the crackling, open fire and smell the tantalizing aromas simmering on the old wood-burning stove as they discussed each special detail of the day.

"He will be here this very morning," the farmer's wife said with a note of excitement in her voice. "We must prepare a breakfast feast with fresh eggs, milk, and ham, befitting a royal king!"

A *king,* thought the gray mare as she excitedly tossed her head from side to side. *I wonder . . . could this be the same king who was born in a lowly manger, just like ours? After all, it is Christmas Day!*

I must return and share this good news with the other animals!

The gray mare's footsteps faltered as she struggled to maintain any rhythm in her gallop. It became obvious to the farmer's wife that something was bothering the gray mare. With concern in her voice, she said to the farmer, "Perhaps we should have her checked."

When the gray mare returned to the barn, the other animals cheered with joy at the news of the pending visit from a king!

The roosting mother hen could hardly contain her excitement as she proudly puffed out her feathers.

"Christmastime is for joyful hearts," she said. "What could be more joyous than sharing a gift from the heart? Why don't we all come up with a Christmas gift that will help the farmer and his wife prepare for their Christmas celebration?"

"Fresh eggs will be my gift? How about the rest of you?"

The caramel-colored dairy cow was next.

She thought for a moment . . . *I know! I will do my best to contribute more refreshing milk than ever before!*

A burst of excitement filled the barn. *What a wonderful plan*, the animals all thought. The rosy-speckled pig was sitting beside the caramel-colored dairy cow. *What could he possibly give*, the animals all wondered.

With despair growing in his heart, the rosy-speckled pig thought, *I have nothing to offer.* How could he possibly match the generosity of the roosting mother hen and the caramel-colored dairy cow?

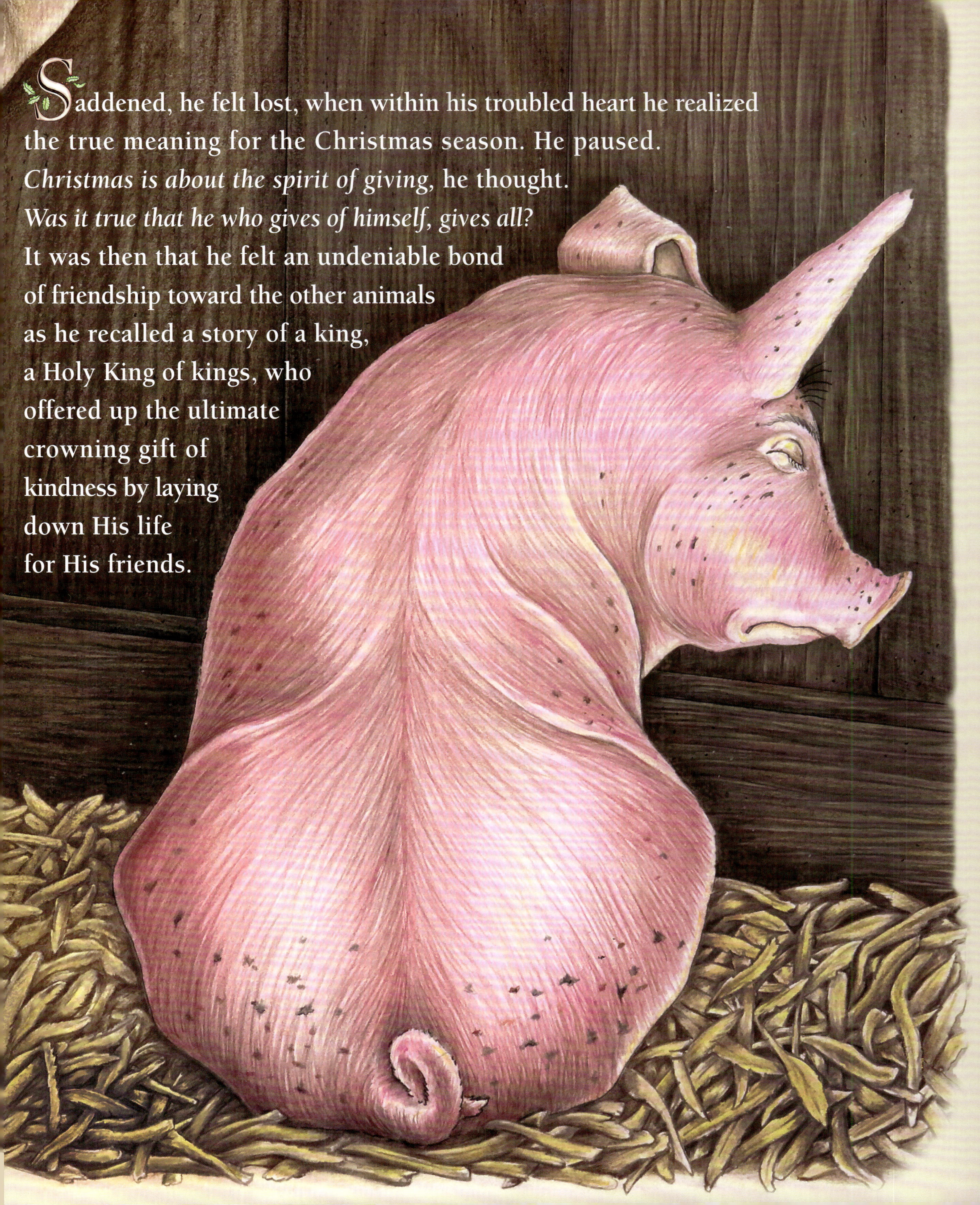

Saddened, he felt lost, when within his troubled heart he realized the true meaning for the Christmas season. He paused. *Christmas is about the spirit of giving,* he thought. *Was it true that he who gives of himself, gives all?* It was then that he felt an undeniable bond of friendship toward the other animals as he recalled a story of a king, a Holy King of kings, who offered up the ultimate crowning gift of kindness by laying down His life for His friends.

A sense of love and warmth overcame the rosy-speckled pig. Within the barn, he had friends. He could not bear to disappoint them, and he knew in his soul what he must do, the sacrifice he must make. He drew in his breath, and his heart plummeted. It was as if his small world was closing in around him.

After what seemed a lifetime, he lowered his head and whispered, “If the roosting mother hen lovingly contributes fresh eggs, and the caramel-colored dairy cow generously offers extra milk, I . . . I . . . I will,” he paused with a lump in his throat. Silence fell over the other animals as they, too, realized his unspoken intention. It was as if unexpected misfortune overshadowed the life-giving warmth of the morning sun. The hope and anticipation of the Christmas Day were gone.

Each of the animals sensed the rosy-speckled pig's pain. They could all see in his eyes the overwhelming anguish of his aching heart as he tried to stammer his plea. But the words never reached his lips. It was within this solemn, breathless stillness that the animals knew what he was trying to say.

It was strange to think that a day that had begun by radiating life and enduring light had now become so awfully bleak. Then, at the very moment when all seemed lost for the rosy-speckled pig, the big

barn door

burst open!

To the rosy-speckled pig's relief, there stood the farmer and his wife, and the much-anticipated visitor. It was difficult to make out the visitor's features with the sun shining behind him in all its glorious splendor. He was dressed in a long overcoat and carried a large black bag.

The visitor then stepped into the shadows and away from the overwhelming brilliance of the sun. He looked familiar, and so did his black bag. He took off his hat and nodded with all the grace of a noble gentleman. A hush fell over the little barn. *Something is not quite right*, the animals thought. *Could this be our royal king?*

Suddenly, like a burst of lightning from heaven, it came to them. *He is the kindly doctor who takes care of us!* They all wondered why he was making his rounds on Christmas Day.

There was something comfortable about the good doctor's genteel nature. Over the years, he had taken such good care of the animals. The doctor turned to the farmer and the farmer's wife. "You have been gracious enough to open your hearts and home to me by sharing your hearty breakfast feast. The least I can do to return the kindness is to examine the animals."

His hands seemed to be filled with compassion as he ran them over the head and nose of the gray mare, examining her with care and detail.

"She seems fine," the doctor told the farmer's wife. "Perhaps her excitement this morning was simply because it is Christmas Day."

He smiled at the gray mare as he turned to look at the other animals. When he caught sight of the rosy-speckled pig, he seemed to sense that something was not quite right.

His quizzical brow creased as he looked down and affectionately stretched his hand toward the rosy-speckled pig.

"Needn't worry, my dear fellow," he said. "It is Christmas Day! All is well."

Eagerly beaming with gratitude, the animals exchanged comforting glances as the good doctor finished his task.

My job here is done," he said with a smile and a kind wave as he, the farmer and the farmer's wife closed the big barn door and strolled away together in the clear, wintry air.

The rosy-speckled pig sat motionless, beaming with excitement as he tried to hide his elation. With a twinkle in his eye, a gentle smile effortlessly spread across his face, showing the emotion within his grateful heart.

The little barn was once again full of sounds as the animals enjoyed the radiant, life-giving warmth of the morning sun.

You see, at that very moment, deep down, the animals all knew what Christmas was really about. You might say it was simply about a selfless gift.

Perhaps the greatest gift of all.

It was, indeed, a grand Christmas Day!

www.TheChristmasMorningGift.com